HOW TO BE a
COURAGEOUS
Girl of God

AN INTERACTIVE JOURNAL INSPIRED BY EXTRAORDINARY WOMEN OF FAITH

SHILOH kidz

An Imprint of Barbour Publishing, Inc.

ISBN 978-1-64352-068-1

Interior illustrations by Heather Burns, Sara Foresti, Isabella Grott, Fabio Mancini, Bonnie Pang, Riley Stark, Lisa Manuzak Wiley, and Rea Zhai

Published by Shiloh Kidz, an imprint of Barbour Publishing, Inc., 1810 Barbour Drive SE, Uhrichsville, Ohio 44683, www.shilohkidz.com

Our mission is to inspire the world with the life-changing message of the Bible.

 Member of the
Evangelical Christian
Publishers Association

Printed in China.

06474 0619 DS

CONTENTS

YOU CAN BE A COURAGEOUS GIRL!

Yes. . .*YOU!*

Featuring brief descriptions of dozens of Bible women, this book will inspire you to become courageous too, as you learn from the examples of strong women of faith—including Abigail, Anna, Deborah, Dorcas, Elizabeth, Mary, and dozens more!

Each section will prompt you to:

1. Read the complete story in your own Bible
2. Draw a related picture
3. Journal your thoughts about courageous women of the Bible
4. Think about how you can be a courageous girl too!

Let's get started! Turn the page to begin your very own courageous journey!

ABIGAIL

READ THE STORY OF ABIGAIL IN YOUR BIBLE. YOU'LL FIND IT IN 1 SAMUEL 25:1–42.

When Abigail's husband, Nabal, was rude to David's men, David became very angry at Nabal and sent more than four hundred soldiers to confront him. . . but before the soldiers got there, Abigail quickly and bravely took action—standing up for what she knew was right. She sent her servants to give David's men food and supplies, and she apologized to David for her husband's bad behavior. Abigail saved the day!

Draw a picture from Abigail's story.

Abigail was courageous because. . .

She stood up for what was
right

I can be a courageous girl of God, like Abigail, when. . .

Some one is mean to me or Others, I can give them grace

When someone does something bad to you, do not pay him back with something bad. Try to do what all men know is right and good.

ROMANS 12:17

ANNA

READ THE STORY OF ANNA IN YOUR BIBLE. YOU'LL FIND IT IN LUKE 2:21–38.

Anna talked with God every day. In fact, she spent most of her life learning God's Word and waiting on the promised Messiah, who would come to save the world from sin. One day when Anna was very old, she saw Baby Jesus in the temple, and she was overjoyed—the Messiah had come! Anna went and shared the good news of Jesus' birth with the people in Jerusalem.

Draw a picture from Anna's story.

Anna was courageous because. . .

_____
_____
_____
_____
_____
_____
_____
_____
_____
_____
_____
_____
_____
_____
_____
_____
_____
_____
_____
_____
_____

I can be a courageous girl of God, like Anna, when. . .

I do everything to spread the Good News and share in its blessings.

1 CORINTHIANS 9:23 NLT

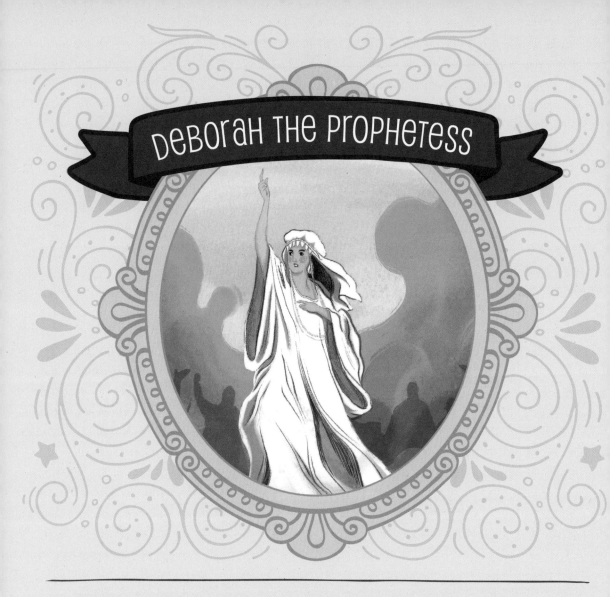

DEBORAH THE PROPHETESS

READ THE STORY OF DEBORAH IN YOUR BIBLE. YOU'LL FIND IT IN JUDGES 4–5.

God trusted Deborah, Israel's only female judge, with a dangerous mission—to free the Israelites from the control of Canaan's cruel king. God wanted His people freed from the king's evil ways. According to Deborah, "The LORD has already cleared the way" (Judges 4:14 NCV). Deborah faced danger to protect the Israelites, and she needed courage for the mission. She fully relied on God to provide it!

Draw a picture from Deborah's story.

Deborah was courageous because. . .

I can be a courageous girl of God, like Deborah, when. . .

"Be strong and courageous, and do the work. Don't be afraid or discouraged, for the LORD God, my God, is with you."

1 CHRONICLES 28:20 NLT

Dorcas

READ THE STORY OF DORCAS IN YOUR BIBLE. YOU'LL FIND IT IN ACTS 9:36–43.

Dorcas was well known among her people as a Jesus follower. She was a talented dressmaker who could have sold her beautiful clothing to the rich, but instead she gave it to the poor. Women who had nothing and were alone caring for their families, and those whose husbands had died, wore Dorcas's beautiful clothes. Dorcas shined her light for Jesus through her many acts of kindness.

Draw a picture from Dorcas's story.

Dorcas was courageous because. . .

I can be a courageous girl of God, like Dorcas, when. . .

God always does what is right. He will not forget the work you did to help the Christians and the work you are still doing to help them. This shows your love for Christ.

HEBREWS 6:10

ELIZABETH

READ THE STORY OF ELIZABETH IN YOUR BIBLE. YOU'LL FIND IT IN LUKE 1.

Elizabeth, who was much too old to have a baby, was quite surprised when an angel shared that she would give birth to a child. But still she trusted in God's plan. The angel said Elizabeth would have a baby boy whom she and her husband should name John. John would be great in the sight of God, he would love God, and he would introduce Jesus to the world. Elizabeth's miracle baby, John the Baptist, was born about six months before Jesus.

Draw a picture from Elizabeth's story.

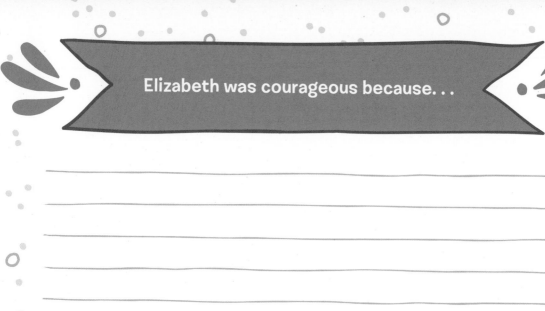

Elizabeth was courageous because. . .

**I can be a courageous girl of God,
like Elizabeth, when. . .**

"For I know the plans I have for you," says the Lord, "plans for well-being and not for trouble, to give you a future and a hope."

JEREMIAH 29:11

ESTHER

READ THE STORY OF ESTHER IN YOUR BIBLE. YOU'LL FIND IT IN ESTHER 2:1–9:25.

Queen Esther had kept a big secret from her husband, the king: she was Jewish. He disliked Jews, and if he had known, he might not have married Esther. When evil Haman convinced the king to order that all the Jews be killed, Esther willingly risked her life to confess the truth and spared the lives of her people. Esther trusted that no matter what happened, God was on her side.

Draw a picture from Esther's story.

Esther was courageous because. . .

I can be a courageous girl of God, like Esther, when. . .

*The Lord hates lying lips, but those
who speak the truth are His joy.*

PROVERBS 12:22

HANNAH

READ THE STORY OF HANNAH IN YOUR BIBLE. YOU'LL FIND IT IN 1 SAMUEL 1:1–2:1, 21.

Hannah was bullied because she didn't have children. But instead of making her bad situation worse, she took her troubles straight to God. She went to the temple and prayed, asking God for a son. Hannah promised that if God gave her a son, she would give the boy back to Him. She would allow him to be raised in the temple so he would grow up to serve God. Because of Hannah's faith, God blessed her with a son, Samuel.

Draw a picture from Hannah's story.

Hannah was courageous because. . .

I can be a courageous girl of God, like Hannah, when. . .

LORD, even when I have trouble all around me,
you will keep me alive. When my enemies are angry,
you will reach down and save me by your power.

PSALM 138:7 NCV

HULDAH

READ THE STORY OF HULDAH IN YOUR BIBLE. YOU'LL FIND IT IN
2 KINGS 22:14–20; 2 CHRONICLES 34:22–33.

Huldah, wife of the king's wardrobe keeper, was a prophetess—a woman with the gift of talking with God and passing His words to the people. King Josiah sent his men to Huldah to ask what God had to say to Jewish people who had been disobedient. The prophetess Huldah listened carefully then shared God's life-changing message with the people of Israel: God was pleased with Josiah and would hold off punishment as long as Josiah lived.

Draw a picture from Huldah's story.

Huldah was courageous because. . .

I can be a courageous girl of God, like Huldah, when. . .

"Call to Me, and I will answer you. And I will show you great and wonderful things which you do not know."

JEREMIAH 33:3

Jairus's Daughter

READ THE STORY OF JAIRUS'S DAUGHTER IN YOUR BIBLE.
YOU'LL FIND IT IN MATTHEW 9:18–25; MARK 5:21–43; LUKE 8:41–56.

Jairus's daughter was twelve years old and very sick. But her father had hope. He trusted that Jesus could heal his daughter, if only he could get to Him and ask. Jairus pushed his way through the crowds that followed Jesus. . .but by the time he got to Jesus, news came that his daughter had died. Jesus followed Jairus home, and with the words "Child, get up!" (Luke 8:54) she was brought back to life.

Draw a picture from Jairus's daughter's story.

Jairus's daughter was courageous because. . .

_____
_____
_____
_____
_____
_____
_____
_____
_____
_____
_____
_____
_____
_____
_____
_____
_____
_____
_____
_____
_____

**I can be a courageous girl of God,
like Jairus's daughter, when. . .**

Be happy in your hope. Do not give up when trouble comes.
Do not let anything stop you from praying.

ROMANS 12:12

JOCHEBED

READ THE STORY OF JOCHEBED IN YOUR BIBLE. YOU'LL FIND IT IN EXODUS 2:1–10.

The Pharaoh, who was not a nice king, worried that the Israelites might become powerful enough to overthrow his government. Each boy baby meant more men to fight in the future. When Pharaoh ruled that all baby boys be put to death, Jochebed, the mother of Baby Moses, was afraid. She created a basket for Moses made from straw and tar and set her baby afloat in the Nile River. Moses was found by Pharaoh's daughter and raised in Pharaoh's palace!

Draw a picture from Jochebed's story.

Jochebed was courageous because. . .

I can be a courageous girl of God, like Jochebed, when. . .

_____

_____

_____

_____

_____

_____

_____

_____

_____

_____

_____

_____

_____

_____

_____

_____

_____

_____

_____

_____

_____

_____

*"For My thoughts are not your thoughts,
and My ways are not your ways,"* says the Lord.

ISAIAH 55:8

_____
_____
_____
_____
_____
_____
_____
_____
_____
_____
_____
_____
_____
_____
_____

LOIS

READ THE STORY OF LOIS IN YOUR BIBLE. YOU'LL FIND IT IN 2 TIMOTHY 1:3–7.

Although she's only mentioned once in the Bible, we know that Timothy's grandmother, Lois, had true faith—and she didn't keep it to herself! She taught Timothy to have that same kind of faith too. Lois was probably like many grandmothers today who love their children, grandchildren—and Jesus!

Draw a picture from Lois's story.

Lois was courageous because. . .

I can be a courageous girl of God, like Lois, when. . .

And so let us come near to God
with a true heart full of faith.
HEBREWS 10:22

LYDIA

READ THE STORY OF LYDIA IN YOUR BIBLE. YOU'LL FIND IT IN ACTS 16:12–15, 40.

Lydia was a business owner in Philippi, which was very unusual for a woman in her day. She was a seller of purple cloth. One day Lydia went with some women to a peaceful area near a river to pray. There she met Timothy and Paul. She listened as Paul talked about Jesus being the only way to heaven. Lydia believed his words, and she invited Jesus into her heart. She became the first Christian in Europe and helped to spread the good news of Jesus!

Draw a picture from Lydia's story.

Lydia was courageous because. . .

_____
_____
_____
_____
_____
_____
_____
_____
_____
_____
_____
_____
_____
_____
_____
_____
_____
_____
_____
_____
_____
_____
_____

**I can be a courageous girl of God,
like Lydia, when. . .**

Let me tell you that the Good News is for the people who are not Jews also. They are able to have life that lasts forever. . . . They are to receive all that God has promised through Christ.

EPHESIANS 3:6

MARY, MOTHER OF JESUS

READ THE STORY OF MARY, MOTHER OF JESUS, IN YOUR BIBLE.
YOU'LL FIND IT IN LUKE 1:26–38.

On a day that started like any other, Mary received an extraordinary greeting from the angel Gabriel. He said, "Don't be afraid, Mary. . . . You will become pregnant and give birth to a son, and you will name him Jesus" (Luke 1:30–31 NCV). Although the angel's message seemed unbelievable, Mary chose to trust God. Mary's obedience set the stage for the birth of Jesus, the Savior of the world!

Draw a picture from Mary's story.

Mary was courageous because. . .

I can be a courageous girl of God, like Mary, when. . .

The Lord is my light and the One Who saves me. Whom should I fear?
The Lord is the strength of my life. Of whom should I be afraid?

PSALM 27:1

MARY MAGDALENE

READ THE STORY OF MARY MAGDALENE IN YOUR BIBLE.
YOU'LL FIND IT IN MARK 16:9; LUKE 8:2; JOHN 20:1–18.

Mary Magdalene became one of Jesus' followers after He healed her. She had been possessed by demons, and Jesus cast them out. Mary was there the day Jesus died on the cross. And three days later, she went to the tomb and discovered Jesus' body was gone! As she cried, she saw Jesus—alive and well! She was the first person to tell others, "He lives!"

Draw a picture from Mary Magdalene's story.

Mary Magdalene was courageous because. . .

I can be a courageous girl of God, like Mary Magdalene, when. . .

God raised Jesus from the dead, and if God's Spirit is living in you, he will also give life to your bodies that die.

ROMANS **8:11** NCV

MARY OF BETHANY

READ THE STORY OF MARY OF BETHANY IN YOUR BIBLE. YOU'LL FIND IT IN JOHN 11:1–44.

Mary of Bethany was hoping Jesus would heal her sick brother, Lazarus, but Jesus didn't show up until after Lazarus had already died. When Jesus arrived and saw how sad His friend was, He cried too. Jesus went to the tomb with Mary and her sister, Martha, where He said, "Lazarus, come out!" Lazarus came out of the tomb, alive and well! Through this miracle, Jesus proved to disbelievers in Bethany that He truly was God's Son!

Draw a picture from Mary of Bethany's story.

Mary of Bethany was courageous because. . .

**I can be a courageous girl of God,
like Mary of Bethany, when. . .**

"God will take away all their tears. There will be no more death or sorrow or crying or pain."

REVELATION 21:4

MIRIAM

READ THE STORY OF MIRIAM IN YOUR BIBLE.
YOU'LL FIND IT IN EXODUS 2; 15:20–21; NUMBERS 12.

When Egypt's pharaoh ordered his men to kill all the Jewish baby boys, Miriam helped to save her baby brother's life. She found a way to keep Moses alive by suggesting to the pharaoh's daughter that she find a Jewish woman to help care for the baby. Because of Miriam's courageous actions, Moses grew up to be a great leader of the Israelites.

Draw a picture from Miriam's story.

Miriam was courageous because. . .

_____
_____
_____
_____
_____
_____
_____
_____
_____
_____
_____
_____
_____
_____
_____
_____
_____
_____

I can be a courageous girl of God, like Miriam, when. . .

"Be strong and have strength of heart. Do not be afraid or shake with fear because of them. For the Lord your God is the One Who goes with you."

DEUTERONOMY **31:6**

NAAMAN'S SERVANT GIRL

READ THE STORY OF NAAMAN'S SERVANT GIRL IN YOUR BIBLE. YOU'LL FIND IT IN 2 KINGS 5.

Naaman, a leader of the Syrian army, had a terrible skin disease. His servant girl said that she knew a man of God who could heal Naaman. So Naaman went to Elisha's door. Elisha, one of God's prophets, told Naaman to wash seven times in the dirty Jordan River. . .and when he did, he was healed! All because a young servant girl had the courage to share her trust in God's mighty power!

Draw a picture from Naaman's servant girl's story.

Naaman's servant girl was courageous because. . .

_____

_____

_____

_____

_____

_____

_____

_____

_____

_____

_____

_____

_____

_____

_____

_____

_____

_____

_____

_____

_____

_____

I can be a courageous girl of God, like Naaman's servant girl, when. . .

A final word: Be strong in the Lord and in his mighty power.

EPHESIANS 6:10 NLT

NAOMI

READ THE STORY OF NAOMI IN YOUR BIBLE. YOU'LL FIND IT IN RUTH 1–4.

After Naomi's husband and sons died, her daughter-in-law, Ruth, insisted on traveling with her from Moab back to her homeland of Bethlehem. They walked fifty miles back to Bethlehem, bringing with them only what they needed for the trip. When they arrived, Ruth went to work, gathering grain from the field of Boaz, who was a relative of Naomi's husband. Ruth and Boaz eventually married, and Naomi had a home with them for the rest of her life.

Draw a picture from Naomi's story.

Naomi was courageous because. . .

I can be a courageous girl of God, like Naomi, when. . .

We know that God makes all things work together for the good of those who love Him and are chosen to be a part of His plan.

ROMANS 8:28

NOAH'S WIFE

READ THE STORY OF NOAH'S WIFE IN YOUR BIBLE.
YOU'LL FIND IT IN GENESIS 6:18; 7:7, 13; 8:16, 19.

The Bible doesn't say much about Noah's wife, but we do know that she must have shared Noah's strong faith and trust in God. Noah's wife believed him when he shared God's plan for building the ark and for saving his family. And so she joined Noah on the big boat (along with their three sons and their wives), trusting that God would save them from the flood.

Draw a picture from Noah's wife's story.

Noah's wife was
courageous because. . .

_____

_____

_____

_____

_____

_____

_____

_____

_____

_____

_____

_____

_____

_____

_____

_____

_____

_____

I can be a courageous girl of God, like Noah's wife, when. . .

What can we say about all these things?
Since God is for us, who can be against us?
ROMANS **8:31**

PETER'S MOTHER-IN-LAW

READ THE STORY OF PETER'S MOTHER-IN-LAW IN YOUR BIBLE.
YOU'LL FIND IT IN MATTHEW 8:14–15; MARK 1:29–31; LUKE 4:38–39.

Peter's mother-in-law was ill. And although she had plenty to do before Jesus and Peter's other friends arrived at her house, she ended up sick in bed, unable to greet them when they came through the door. Jesus showed her loving-kindness and healed her so she could get up and accomplish what she wanted to do—care for the needs of others.

Draw a picture from Peter's mother-in-law's story.

Peter's mother-in-law was
courageous because. . .

I can be a courageous girl of God, like Peter's mother-in-law, when. . .

He gives strength to the weak. And He gives power to him who has little strength.

Isaiah 40:29

PRISCILLA

READ THE STORY OF PRISCILLA IN YOUR BIBLE. YOU'LL FIND IT IN ACTS 18:1–3, 18–28.

Tentmakers Priscilla and her husband, Aquila, became close friends with Paul, who was also a tentmaker. In Corinth, they spent lots of time together, making tents and talking about the Bible. When Paul decided to move on, Priscilla and her husband decided to travel with him, and they shared the good news of Jesus wherever they went.

Draw a picture from Priscilla's story.

Priscilla was courageous because...

I can be a courageous girl of God, like Priscilla, when. . .

> *Some friends may ruin you, but a real friend*
> *will be more loyal than a brother.*
> PROVERBS **18:24** NCV

THE PROVERBS 31 WOMAN

READ THE STORY OF THE PROVERBS 31 WOMAN IN YOUR BIBLE.
YOU'LL FIND IT IN PROVERBS 31:10–31.

A Proverbs 31 woman knows how to manage finances. If she chooses to work, she does and brings money into the household. She stays up late at night caring for her family, and still she finds time to take care of herself. Most important, she loves and respects God, and others see Him through her. She is wise and helps her neighbors, the poor, and the needy. According to God's Word, a good wife and mom is worth more than rubies!

Draw a picture from the Proverbs 31 Woman's story.

The Proverbs 31 Woman was courageous because. . .

**I can be a courageous girl of God,
like the Proverbs 31 Woman, when. . .**

She is strong and is respected by the people.
She looks forward to the future with joy.

PROVERBS 31:25 NCV

RAHAB

READ THE STORY OF RAHAB IN YOUR BIBLE. YOU'LL FIND IT IN JOSHUA 2; 6:17, 22–23.

Rahab hadn't lived a godly life, but God needed her to help His people. She hid Israelite spies in her house. When it was safe for the spies to leave, Rahab reminded them she had saved their lives. "So now, promise me before the LORD," she said, "that you will show kindness to my family just as I showed kindness to you" (Joshua 2:12 NCV). The spies stayed true to their word, and the lives of Rahab and her family were spared.

Draw a picture from Rahab's story.

Rahab was courageous because. . .

I can be a courageous girl of God, like Rahab, when. . .

It is better not to make a promise,
than to make a promise and not pay it.
ECCLESIASTES 5:5

RHODA

READ THE STORY OF RHODA IN YOUR BIBLE. YOU'LL FIND IT IN ACTS 12:1–17.

Peter, who had been locked up in prison for talking about Jesus, was freed by an angel and went directly to Rhoda's house. When she heard Peter's knock and his voice, she became so excited that she ran to tell the others without opening the door and letting Peter in! She was overcome with pure joy!

Draw a picture from Rhoda's story.

Rhoda was courageous because. . .

I can be a courageous girl of God, like Rhoda, when. . .

"Be like servants who are waiting for their master to come home from a wedding party. When he comes and knocks, the servants immediately open the door for him."

LUKE **12:36** NCV

RUTH

READ THE STORY OF RUTH IN YOUR BIBLE. YOU'LL FIND IT IN RUTH 1:1–18.

After Ruth's husband and father-in-law died, she honored her mother-in-law, Naomi, by traveling with her from Moab to her homeland of Bethlehem. Ruth willingly left the place she had lived her entire life so Naomi wouldn't be alone. Ruth spoke these words: "Where you go, I will go. Where you live, I will live. Your people will be my people, and your God will be my God. And where you die, I will die, and there I will be buried" (Ruth 1:16–17 NCV).

Draw a picture from Ruth's story.

Ruth was courageous because. . .

_____

_____

_____

_____

_____

_____

_____

_____

_____

_____

_____

_____

_____

_____

_____

_____

_____

_____

_____

_____

_____

I can be a courageous girl of God, like Ruth, when. . .

*If you respect your father and mother, you will live
a long time and your life will be full of many good things.*

EPHESIANS 6:3

SAMSON'S MOTHER

READ THE STORY OF SAMSON'S MOTHER IN YOUR BIBLE. YOU'LL FIND IT IN JUDGES 13:1–24.

Samson's mom was visited by an angel of the Lord. The angel told her that she would soon have a son. The angel said that her son would grow up to help set the Israelites free from their enemies, the Philistines. And though her husband didn't completely believe what she told him at first, Samson's mom trusted that what God said was true.

Draw a picture from Samson's mother's story.

Samson's mother was courageous because. . .

_____

_____

_____

_____

_____

_____

_____

_____

_____

_____

_____

_____

_____

_____

_____

_____

_____

_____

_____

_____

_____

_____

_____

**I can be a courageous girl of God,
like Samson's mother, when. . .**

"Whoever can be trusted with a little can also be trusted with a lot, and whoever is dishonest with a little is dishonest with a lot."

Luke 16:10 NCV

Sarah

READ THE STORY OF SARAH IN YOUR BIBLE.
YOU'LL FIND IT IN GENESIS 17:15–17, 19; 18:10–15; 21:1–7.

Sarah was ninety years old when God promised her that she and her husband, Abraham, would have a son. And what did Sarah do when she received the news? She laughed! After all, at her advanced age, the news seemed quite funny! But as always, God's promise came true when, a year later, Sarah gave birth to a baby boy. And she laughed once more. . .but this time with joy that God, in His power, can do the impossible!

Draw a picture from Sarah's story.

Sarah was courageous because. . .

I can be a courageous girl of God, like Sarah, when. . .

"For God can do all things."
LUKE 1:37

SHIPHRAH AND PUAH

READ THE STORY OF SHIPHRAH AND PUAH IN YOUR BIBLE.
YOU'LL FIND IT IN EXODUS 1:8–21.

Shiphrah and Puah were midwives—nurses who helped women when they had babies. One day Pharaoh said to them, "When an Israelite woman gives birth, if the baby is a girl, let her live. If it's a boy, kill him!" Shiphrah and Puah secretly allowed the baby boys to live and their mothers to hide them. God blessed Shiphrah and Puah for obeying Him. He gave them families of their own. And because of these two nurses, the Israelites grew in number.

Draw a picture from Shiphrah and Puah's story.

Shiphrah and Puah were courageous because. . .

_____

_____

_____

_____

_____

_____

_____

_____

_____

_____

_____

_____

_____

_____

_____

_____

_____

_____

_____

_____

**I can be a courageous girl of God,
like Shiphrah and Puah, when. . .**

It is a hated thing for kings to do what is wrong.
For a throne is built on what is right.
PROVERBS **16:12**

THE SHUNAMMITE WOMAN

READ THE STORY OF THE SHUNAMMITE WOMAN IN YOUR BIBLE.
YOU'LL FIND IT IN 2 KINGS 4:8–37.

The Shunammite woman blessed Elisha when he was in her village—making food for him to eat and giving him a place to stay. Because of her hospitality, Elisha wanted to do something for the woman. He learned that she and her husband didn't have a son. Elisha told her, "At this time next year you will hold a son in your arms" (2 Kings 4:16). And God made sure it was so!

Draw a picture from the Shunammite woman's story.

The Shunammite woman was courageous because. . .

I can be a courageous girl of God, like the Shunammite woman, when. . .

"You will be a blessing to others."

GENESIS **12:2** NCV

THE WIDOW OF ZAREPHATH

READ THE STORY OF THE WIDOW OF ZAREPHATH IN YOUR BIBLE.
YOU'LL FIND IT IN 1 KINGS 17:7–16.

During a time of famine (a time when food is hard to get), God told his prophet Elijah there was a widow in Zarephath who would take care of him. When Elijah arrived and asked the widow for food and water, she had only a handful of flour left in a jar and a little olive oil—just enough for one last meal for her and her son. She took care of Elijah, and in the process, her flour and oil never ran out. God saw to it that she had enough to eat!

Draw a picture from the widow of Zarephath's story.

The widow of Zarephath was courageous because. . .

**I can be a courageous girl of God,
like the widow of Zarephath, when. . .**

"I will answer them before they even call to me. While they are still talking about their needs, I will go ahead and answer their prayers!"

Isaiah 65:24 NLT

THE WIDOW WHO GAVE TWO MITES

READ THE STORY OF THE WIDOW WHO GAVE TWO MITES IN YOUR BIBLE.
YOU'LL FIND IT IN MARK 12:41–44; LUKE 21:1–4.

Jesus sat in the temple watching people put money into the money box (kind of like the offering plates passed in churches today). The rich people gave a lot, but they had plenty left over. A poor widow entered the temple and put two mites into the box—giving all she had to live on. Jesus noticed the sacrifice she had made, and He used this widow's story to teach His followers about true giving.

Draw a picture from "the widow who gave two mites" story.

The widow who gave two mites was courageous because. . .

**I can be a courageous girl of God,
like the widow who gave two mites, when. . .**

Each man should give as he has decided in his heart. . . .
God loves a man who gives because he wants to give.
2 CORINTHIANS 9:7

THE WOMAN AT THE WELL

READ THE STORY OF THE WOMAN AT THE WELL IN YOUR BIBLE.
YOU'LL FIND IT IN JOHN 4:4–15.

On His way to Galilee, Jesus stopped and asked a Samaritan woman for water. Jesus offered her "living water" and said, "Everyone who drinks from this well will be thirsty again. But the living water I give will fill you up so you will never be thirsty—and it will give you forever life." The woman said, "Then give me this water!" This was Jesus' way of hinting at what was to come. After He died for our sins, anyone who trusted in Jesus would be filled with God's Spirit (Jesus compared it to "living water") and have never-ending life in heaven.

Draw a picture from the woman at the well's story.

The woman at the well was courageous because. . .

**I can be a courageous girl of God,
like the woman at the well, when. . .**

"For God so loved the world that He gave His only Son. Whoever puts his trust in God's Son will not be lost but will have life that lasts forever."

JOHN 3:16

THE WOMAN WHO ANOINTED JESUS' FEET

READ THE STORY OF THE WOMAN WHO ANOINTED JESUS'
FEET IN YOUR BIBLE. YOU'LL FIND IT IN LUKE 7:36–50.

A woman in the village knew that Jesus was at the home of an important man, so she went there—likely uninvited. The man wasn't happy when she showed up. This woman loved Jesus, and when she saw Him, she cried. Her tears wet Jesus' feet, so she dried them with her long hair. She poured perfume on Jesus' feet and kissed them. How did Jesus respond to the man? "When I got here, you didn't wash My feet, put perfume on them, or kiss them," Jesus said. "This woman loves Me, and her sins are forgiven."

Draw a picture from "the woman who anointed Jesus' feet" story.

The woman who anointed Jesus' feet was courageous because...

I can be a courageous girl of God, like the woman who anointed Jesus' feet, when. . .

> *If we tell Him our sins, He is faithful and we can depend on Him to forgive us of our sins. He will make our lives clean from all sin.*
> 1 JOHN 1:9

THE WOMAN WHO TOUCHED JESUS' COAT

READ THE STORY OF THE WOMAN WHO TOUCHED JESUS' COAT IN YOUR BIBLE. YOU'LL FIND IT IN MATTHEW 9:20–22; MARK 5:25–34; LUKE 8:43–48.

A woman, sick for twelve long years with a bleeding disorder, had tried everything to get well. Nothing had worked. . .and Jesus was her final hope. Pushing her way through a crowd to get to Jesus, she reached out and touched His coat. When she made contact with Jesus, her body was immediately healed! Jesus said, "Daughter, your faith has healed you. Go in peace and be free from your sickness" (Mark 5:34).

Draw a picture from "the woman who touched Jesus' coat" story.

The woman who touched Jesus' coat was courageous because. . .

_____

_____

_____

_____

_____

_____

_____

_____

_____

_____

_____

_____

_____

_____

_____

_____

_____

_____

_____

_____

_____

I can be a courageous girl of God, like the woman who touched Jesus' coat, when. . .

Keep a strong hold on your faith in Christ.

1 TIMOTHY 1:19

MORE IN THE COURAGEOUS GIRLS SERIES!

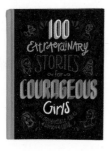

100 Extraordinary Stories for Courageous Girls

Girls are world-changers! And this deeply inspiring storybook proves it! This collection of 100 extraordinary stories of women of faith—from the Bible, history, and today—will empower you to know and understand how women have made a difference in the world and how much smaller our faith (and the biblical record) would be without them.

Hardback / 978-1-68322-748-9 / $16.99

Cards of Kindness for Courageous Girls: Shareable Devotions and Inspiration

You will delight in spreading kindness and inspiration wherever you go with these shareable Cards of Kindness! Each perforated page features a just-right-sized devotional reading plus a positive life message that will both uplift and inspire your young heart.

Paperback / 978-1-64352-164-0 / $7.99

The Bible for Courageous Girls

Part of the exciting "Courageous Girls" book line, this Bible provides complete Old and New Testament text in the easy-reading New Life™ Version, plus insert pages featuring full-color illustrations of bold, brave women such as Abigail, Deborah, Esther, Mary Magdalene, and Mary, mother of Jesus.

DiCarta / 978-1-64352-069-8 / $24.99